ARTIST TRANSCRIPTIONS WOODWINDS

THE ERIC DOLPHY COLLECTION

Transcribed by Robert Duboff and Travis Sullivan

ISBN 0-7935-8637-2

HAL•LEONARD® CORPORATION

7777 W. BLUEMOUND RD. P.O. BOX 13819 MILWAUKEE, WI 53213

Visit Hal Leonard Online at
www.halleonard.com

CONTENTS

BIOGRAPHY

While the average non-jazz fan may be able to name Miles Davis and Charlie Parker as giants of the genre, and possibly recognize the names of John Coltrane or Dizzy Gillespie when heard, you can rest assured they've never heard of Eric Dolphy. In the world of jazz, however, Dolphy's legacy is huge. Revered by several jazz icons, including Charles Mingus and John Coltrane, as an unmatched talent, Dolphy's contributions to the genre are perhaps more alive and inspiring than ever, even thirty-five years after his death. Known for his constant, relentless practicing, he was a virtuoso on alto sax, bass clarinet, and flute and is largely credited for popularizing the latter two as jazz solo instruments. As with countless other jazz legends, including the likes of Charlie "Bird" Parker and Wes Montgomery, Eric Dolphy was taken from us at a very young age. Though the volume of work he did leave behind is no doubt impressive, we will sadly never know the music he still had left to give.

Born in Los Angeles in 1928, Eric Dolphy spent years playing in local L.A. bands before joining Roy Porter's Orchestra in 1948. Though he was not featured as a soloist, his first recorded work can be heard with this band. Beginning in 1950, Dolphy served in the army for two years, playing in the jazz band. After playing in more local bands around Los Angeles for several more years, he joined Chico Hamilton's Quintet in 1958. In this band, which featured a slightly unusual line-up of cello, guitar, bass, and drums, Dolphy could be heard on flute, clarinet, bass clarinet, and alto sax.

After relocating to New York in 1959, he joined the Charles Mingus' Quintet and was featured exclusively. It was through this opportunity that he began to gain much exposure, and eventually, by 1960, began recording regularly for Prestige as a leader. Criticized regularly for his stylistic leanings towards "free jazz," however, Dolphy constantly struggled with finding regular work.

The years of 1960-61 were particularly productive, producing albums with trumpeter Booker Little, Ornette Coleman, and Max Roach, among others. Dolphy joined Coltrane's quintet in late '61 for a European tour, which, due to the lengthy, free-style solos, was subsequently labeled by many critics as "anti-jazz." Following in 1962-63, he played "Third Stream Music" with Gunther Schuller and Orchestra U.S.A., a music aimed at bridging the styles of jazz and classical.

In 1964 Dolphy recorded *Out to Lunch*, a classic album on the Blue Note label. Shortly thereafter he joined Mingus again to record in Europe, resulting in *The Great Concert of Charles Mingus*. Months later, he died suddenly on June 29, 1964, from complications attributed to misdiagnosed diabetes. He was 36 years old.

Apart from his music, Dolphy was known by his peers as a kind and humble person. Mingus, generally not known for handing out compliments, labeled him "a saint." In a profession often filled with substance abuse, Dolphy never touched alcohol or drugs. He instead devoted his time to practicing and more practicing. Since his death, his music has inspired countless young musicians and continues to earn new fans all the time. A nine-CD boxed set, *Eric Dolphy: The Complete Prestige Recordings*, has since been released, which catalogues most of his recording career.

APRIL FOOL

Flute

By ERIC DOLPHY

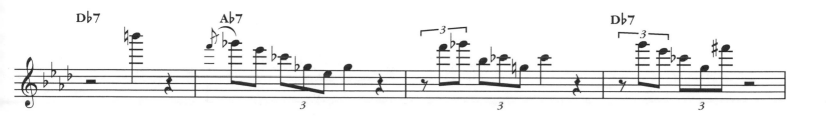

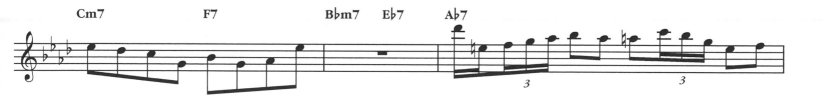

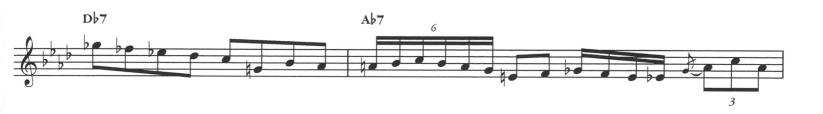

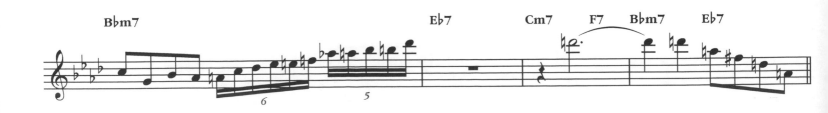

*play harmonic

Begin Fade

Fade out

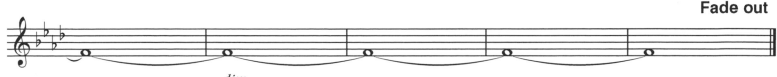

BEMOANABLE LADY

Alto Sax

By CHARLES MINGUS

F9♯5

E9♯5

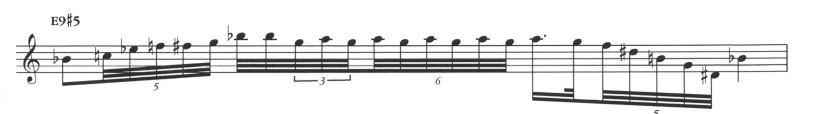

E♭9♯5

D9♯5

D♭9♯5

C9♯5

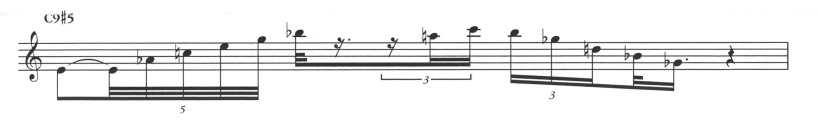

Gm11   **G♭7**   **Fmaj13**

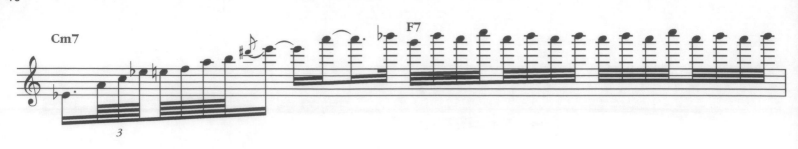

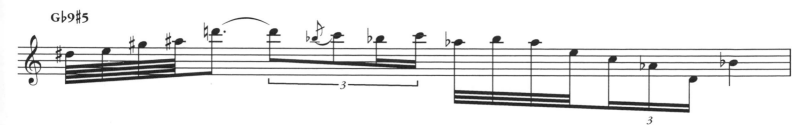

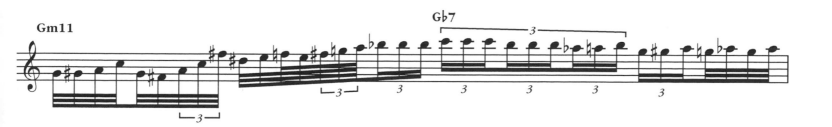

GLAD TO BE UNHAPPY

from ON YOUR TOES

Alto Sax

Words by LORENZ HART
Music by RICHARD RODGERS

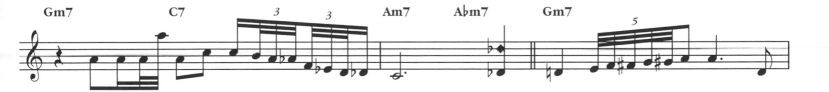

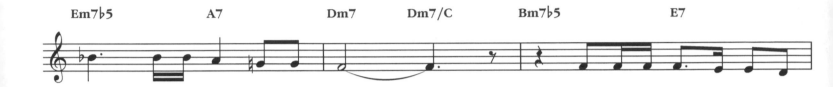

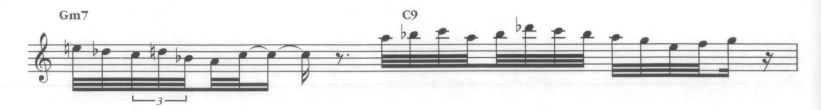

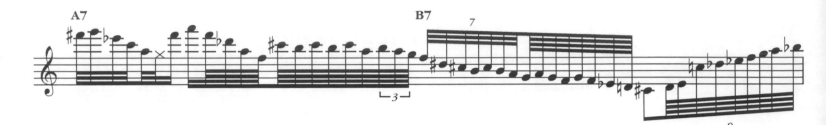

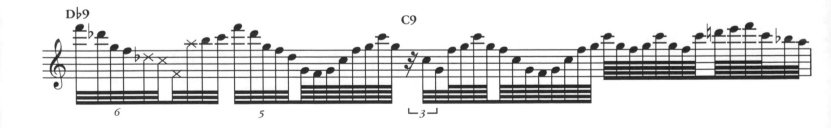

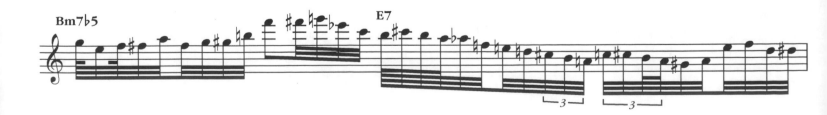

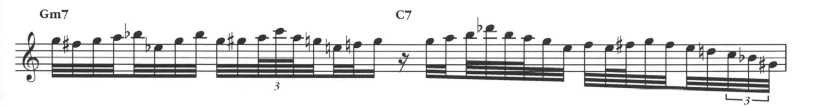

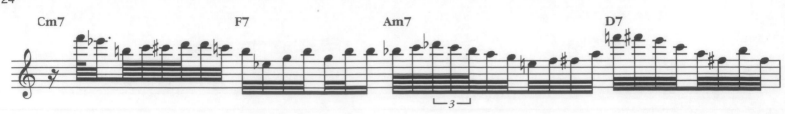

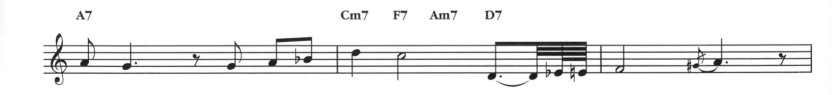

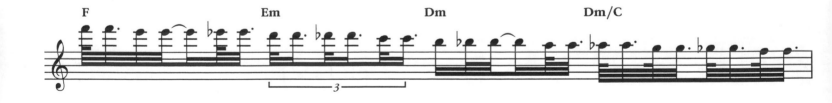

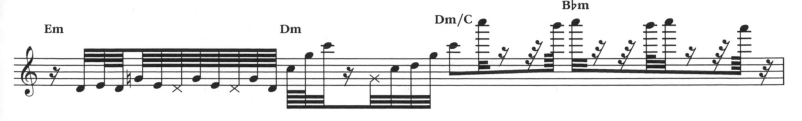

BEYOND THE BLUE HORIZON

from the Paramount Picture MONTE CARLO

Flute

Words by LEO ROBIN
Music by RICHARD A. WHITING
and W. FRANKE HARLING

Guitar 5 **Flute Solo**
Break

Fmaj7

Eb6   Fmaj7

Am7   D7

Gm   C7   Fmaj7

Gm7   C7

Fmaj7   Fmaj7

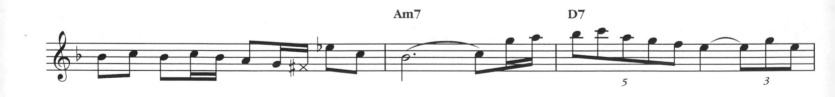

GOD BLESS' THE CHILD

Bass Clarinet

Words and Music by ARTHUR HERZOG JR.
and BILLIE HOLIDAY

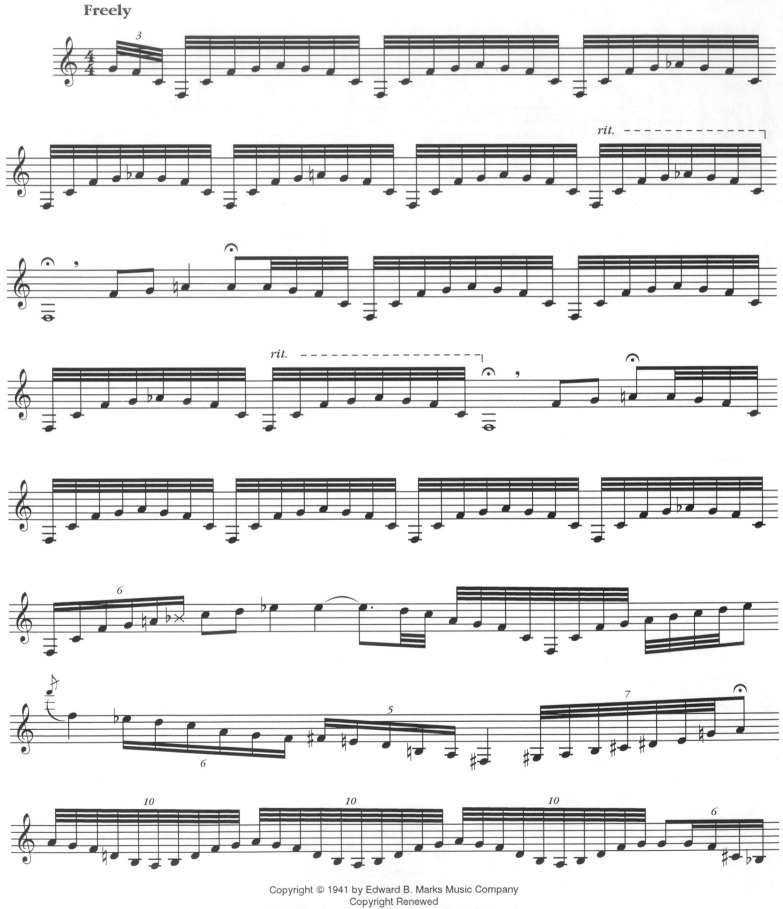

35

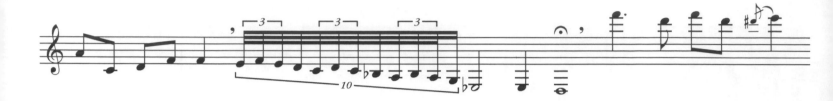

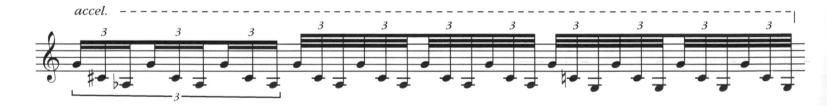

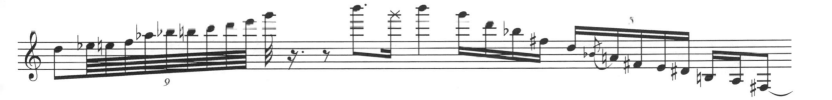

rit. - - - - - - - *accel.*

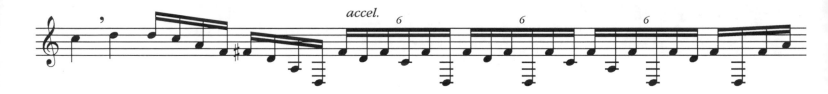

accel.

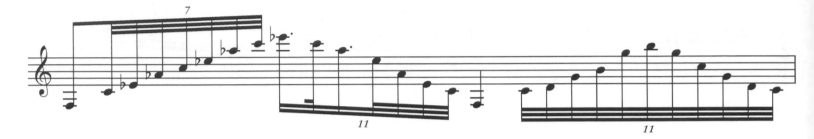

TENDERLY

from TORCH SONG

Alto Sax

Lyric by JACK LAWRENCE
Music by WALTER GROSS

Rubato

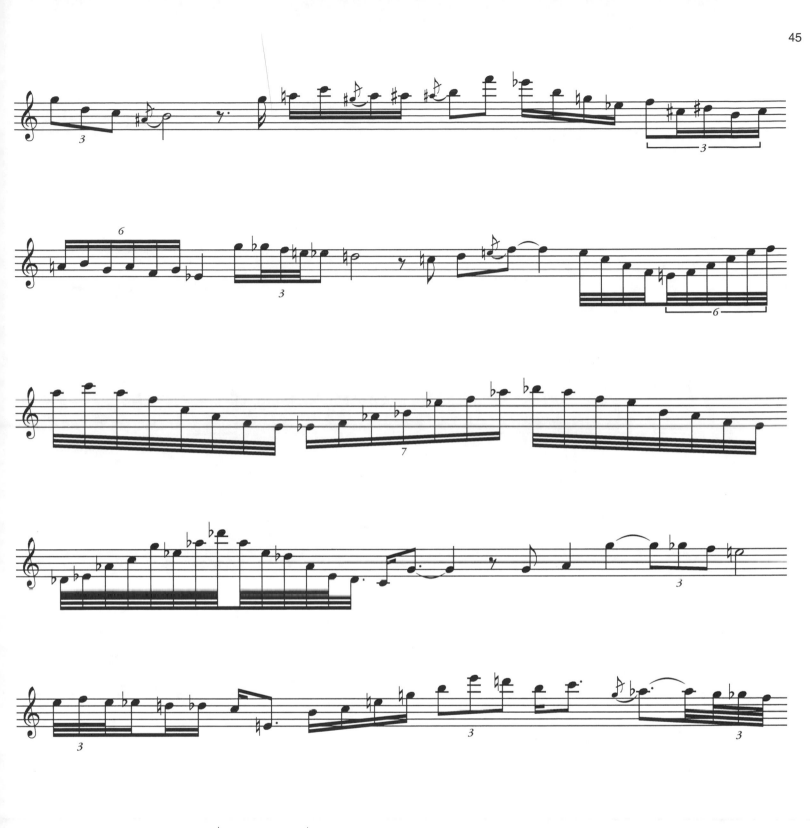

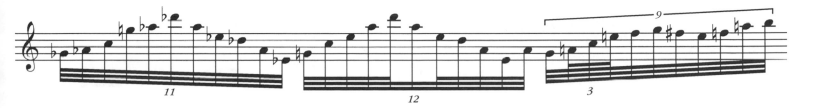

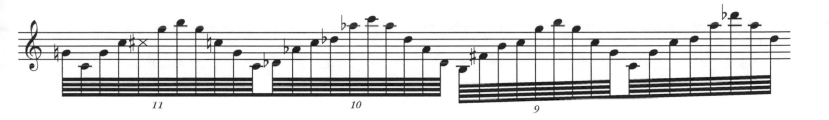

G.W.

Eb Alto Saxophone

By ERIC DOLPHY

Medium Up Tempo Swing ♩ = ca.200

51

Dm11 · Db/F

C#7alt · To Coda ✛ · F7alt

Bbmaj7

Ab7 · E+7

Dm7 · slide - - - - - - - C#m7

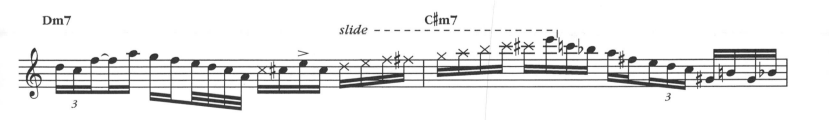

F#7 · Bm7 · E7

play harm.

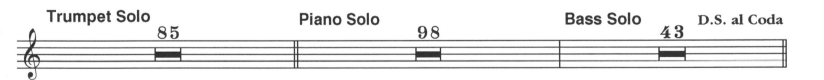

LIKE SOMEONE IN LOVE

Flute

Words by JOHNNY BURKE
Music by JIMMY VAN HEUSEN

Background (Trumpet plays melody)

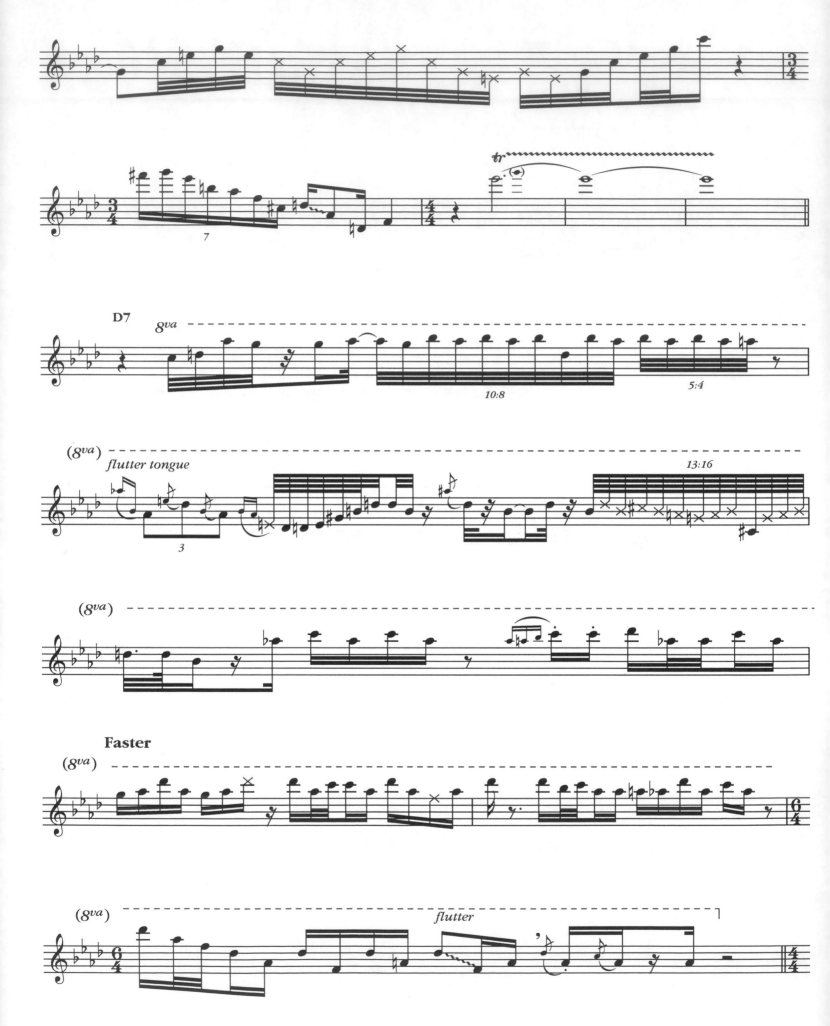

Medium Swing ♩ = 114

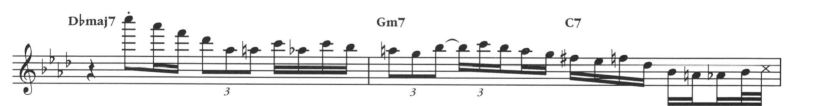

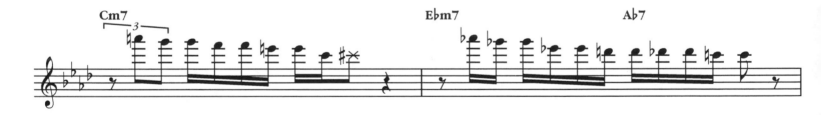

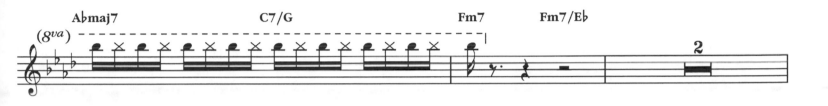

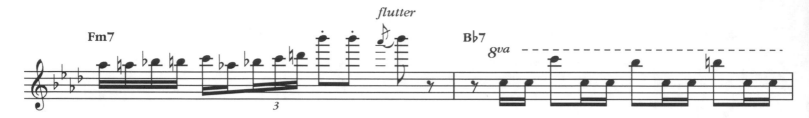

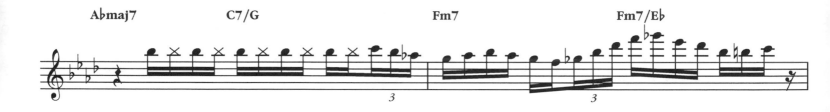

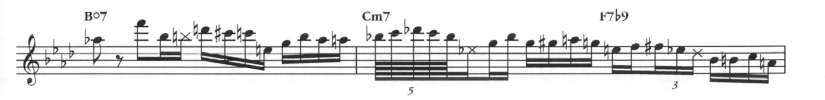

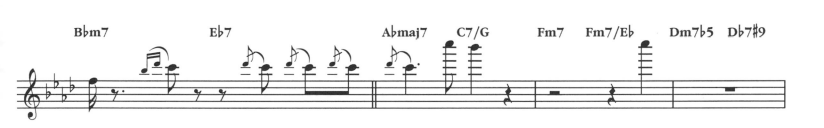

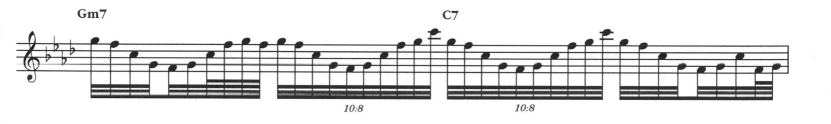

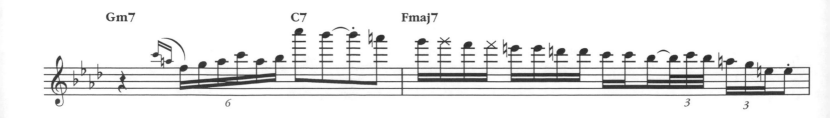

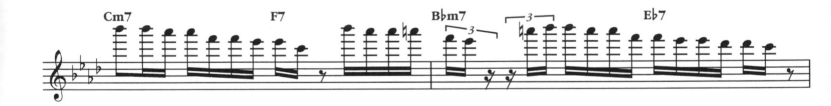

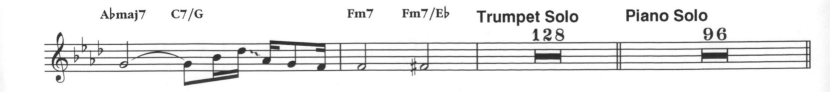

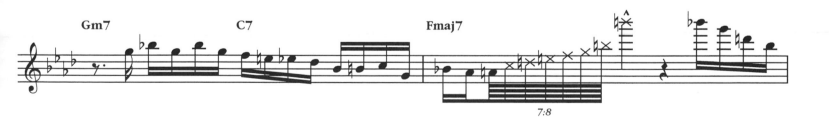

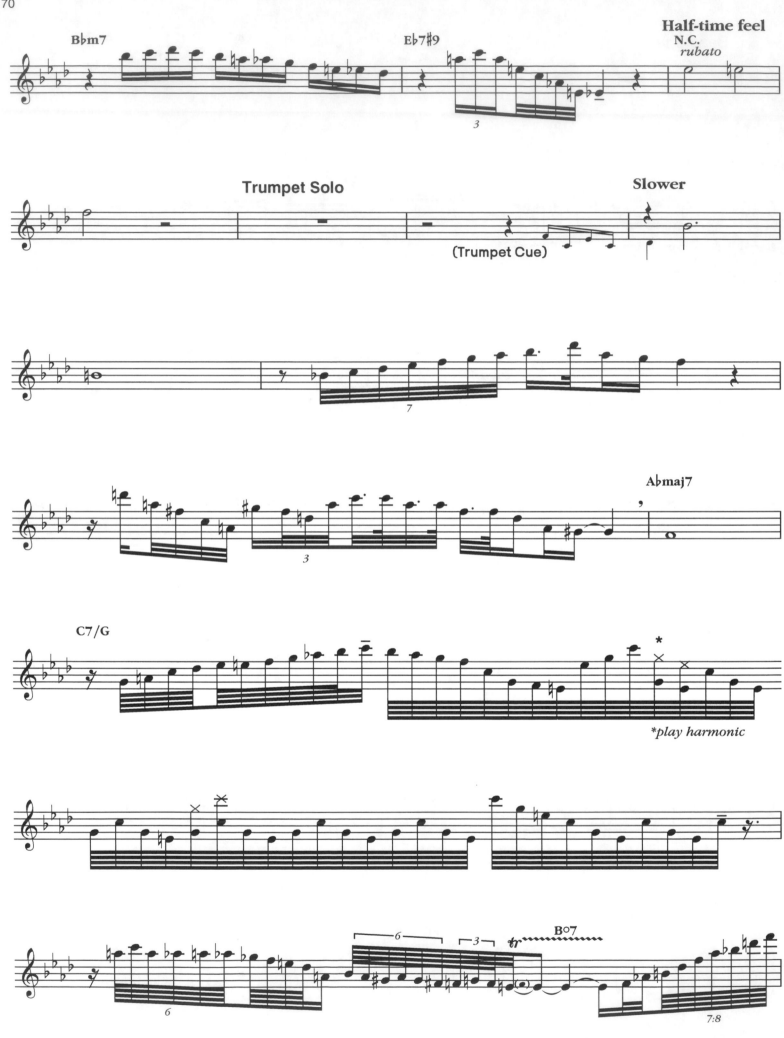

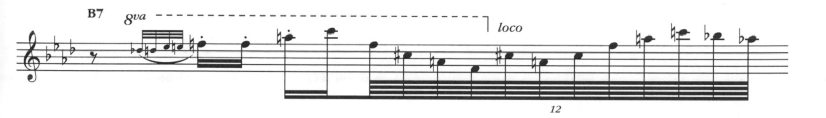

SERENE

B♭ Bass Clarinet

By ERIC DOLPHY

73

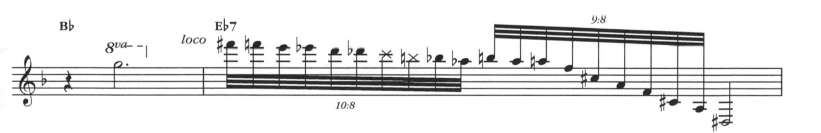

74

*note bend

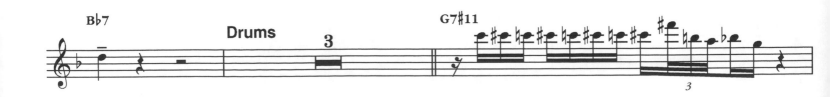

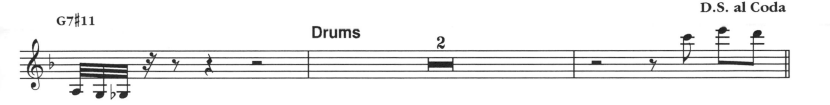

SOFTLY AS IN A MORNING SUNRISE

from THE NEW MOON

Eb Alto Saxophone

Lyrics by OSCAR HAMMERSTEIN II
Music by SIGMUND ROMBERG

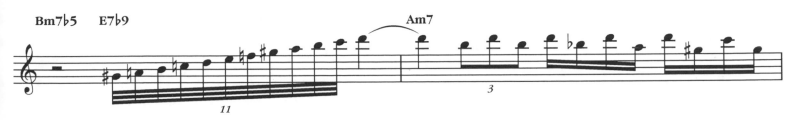

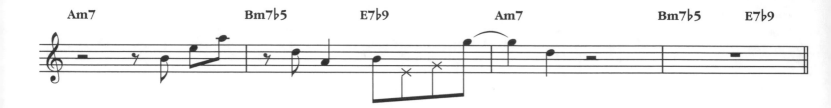

Dm7

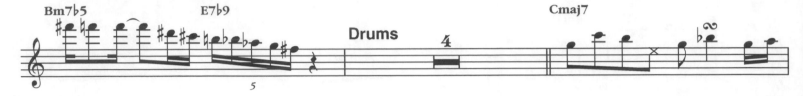

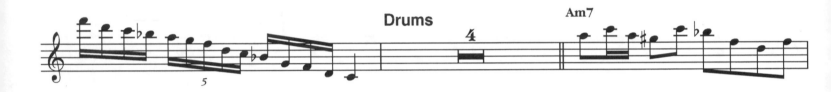

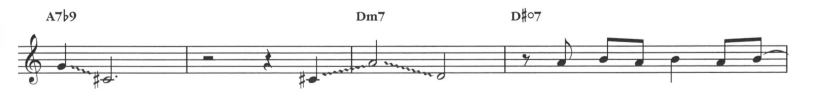

STORMY WEATHER
(KEEPS RAININ' ALL THE TIME)

E♭ Alto Saxophone

Lyric by TED KOEHLER
Music by HAROLD ARLEN

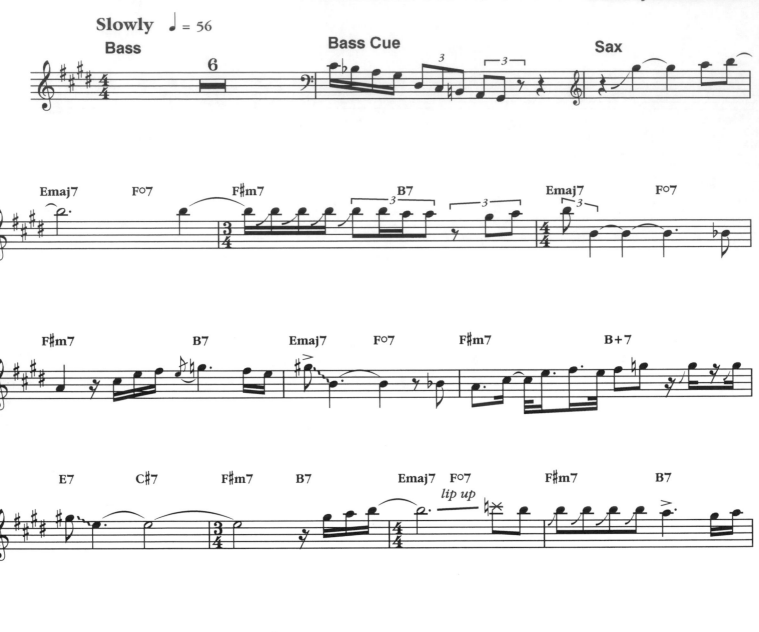

no tongue (lip slur)

*note bend

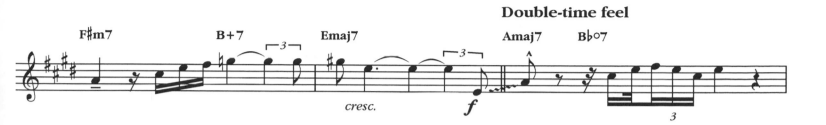

Double-time feel

cresc. *f*

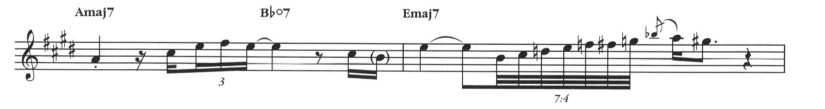

*Finger E and press low B♭ key

lip bend

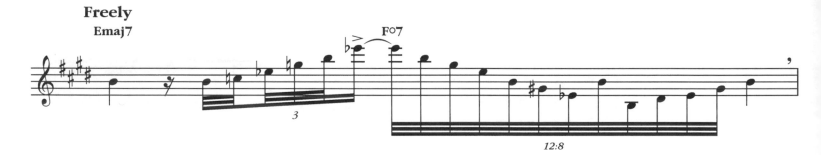

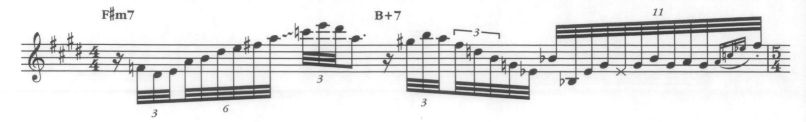

Bass fill   *a tempo*

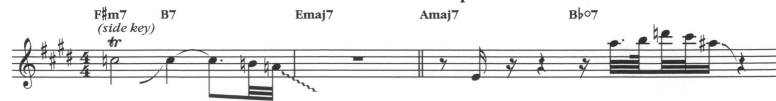

Emaj7

Amaj7   **Bb°7**

Emaj7

Amaj7

Bb°7

Fmaj7

Freely

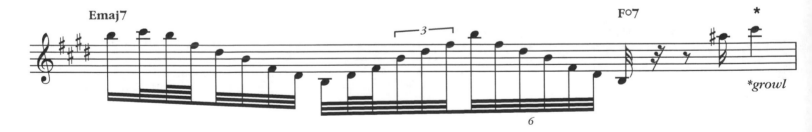

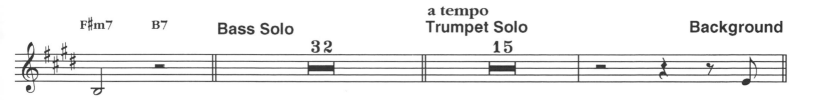

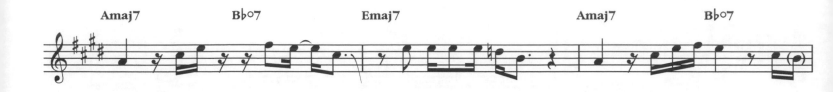

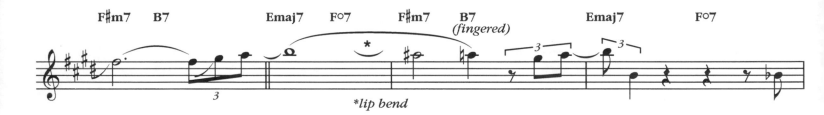

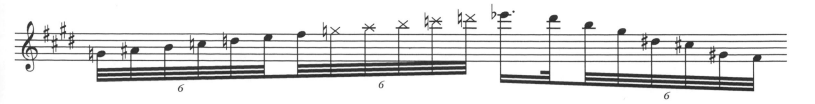

245

Alto Sax

By ERIC DOLPHY

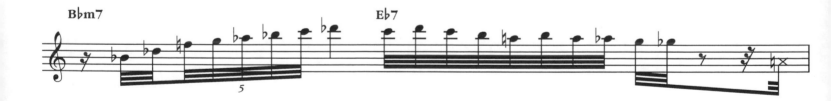

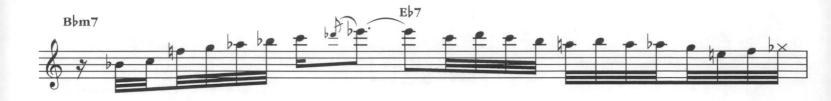

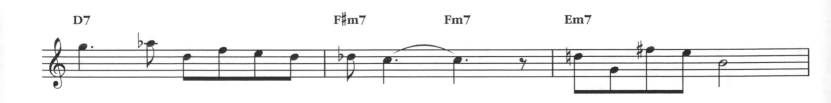

THE WAY YOU LOOK TONIGHT

from SWING TIME

Eb Alto Saxophone

Words by DOROTHY FIELDS
Music by JEROME KERN

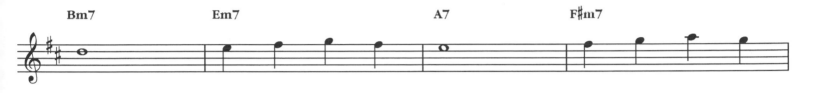

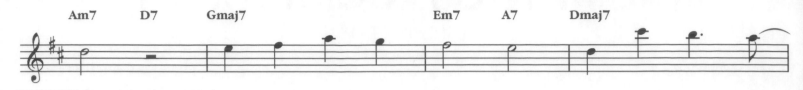

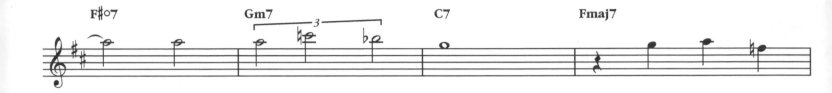

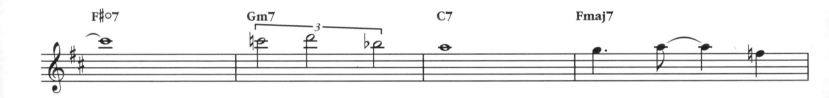

Solo Break

Dmaj7

Gm7 **C7** **Fmaj7** **F#o7**

Gm7 **C7**

Fmaj7 **Dm7**

Gm7 **C7** **Fmaj7**

F#o7 **Gm7** **C7**

Fmaj7 **Em7**

A7 **Dmaj7** **Bm7**

106

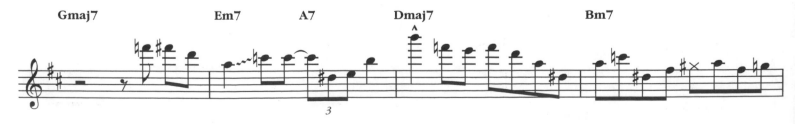

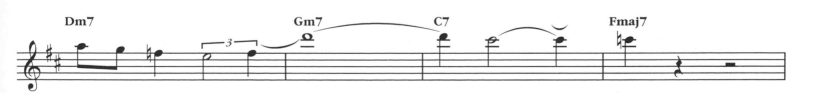

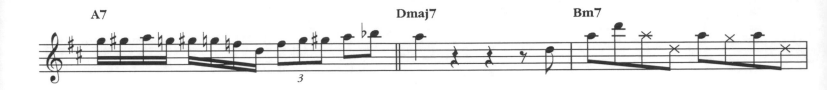

*harm.

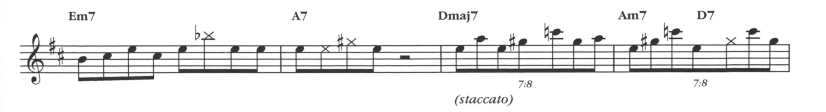

(staccato)

(not staccato)

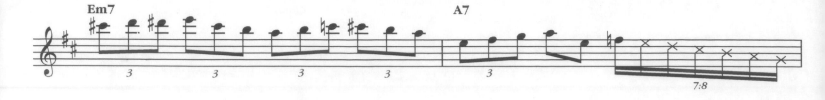

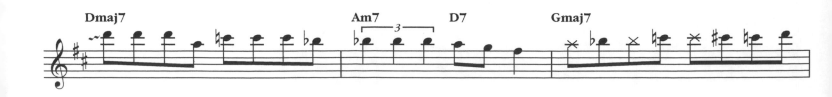

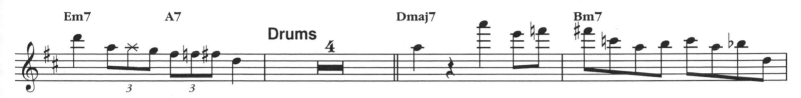

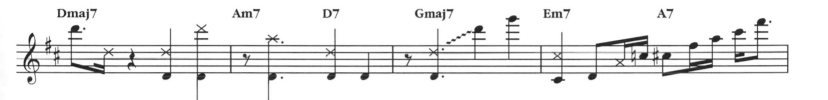
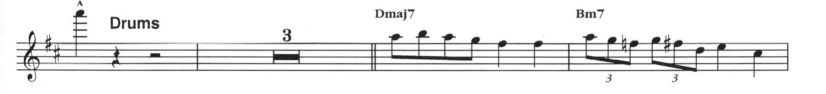

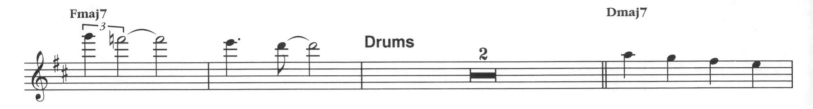

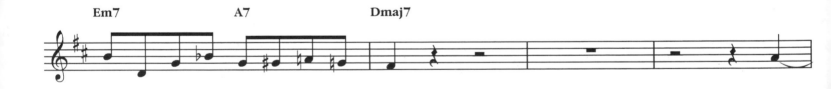

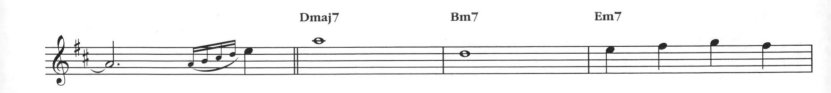

115

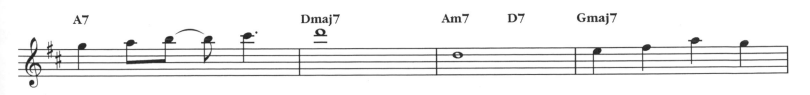

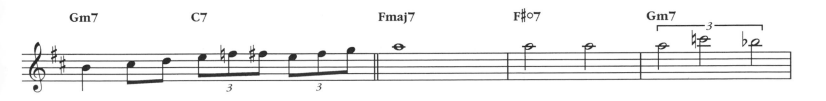

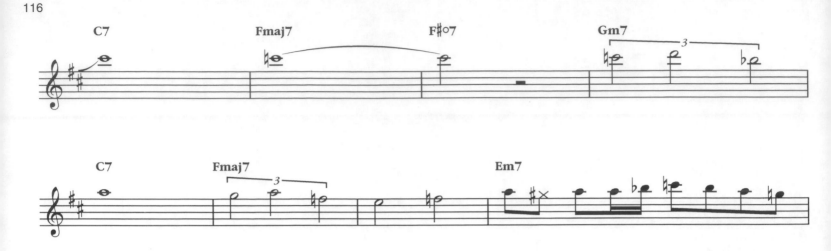

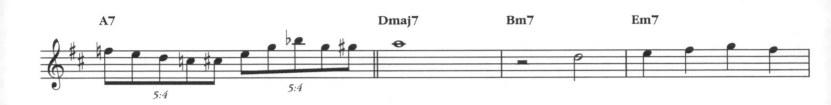

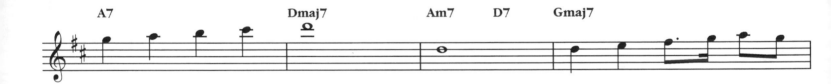

WOODYN' YOU

Eb Alto Sax

By DIZZY GILLESPIE

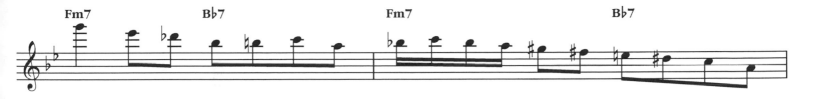

122

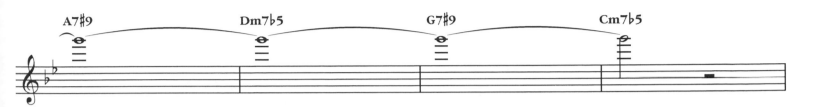

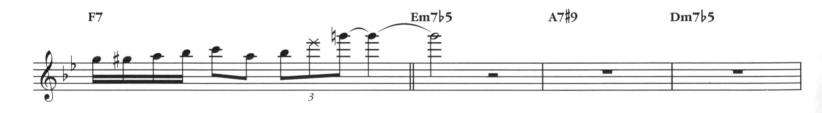

128

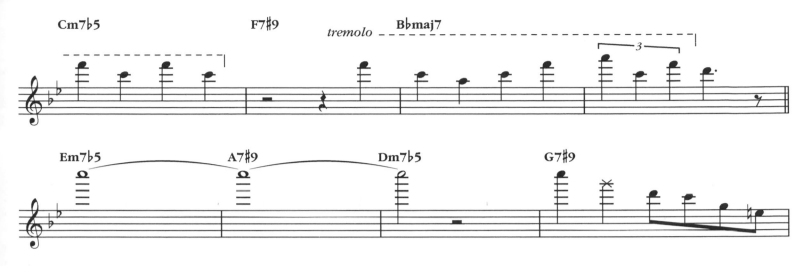

Piano Solo

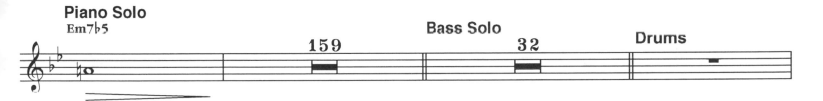

Drums

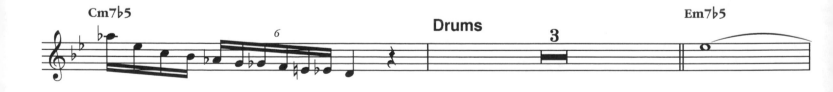

134

Cadenza

YOU DON'T KNOW WHAT LOVE IS

Flute

Words and Music by DON RAYE
and GENE DePAUL

Abmaj7

Slow - rubato

Bbm7

Eb7sus4

Abmaj7

Dm7

G7

Cmaj7

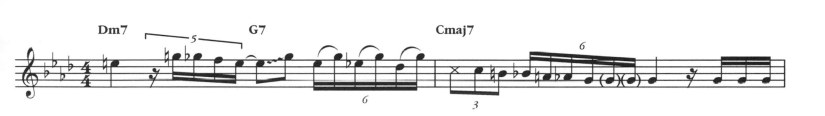

Db9

C7b9

Fm7

Band enters

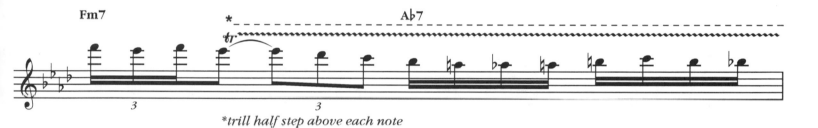

*trill half step above each note

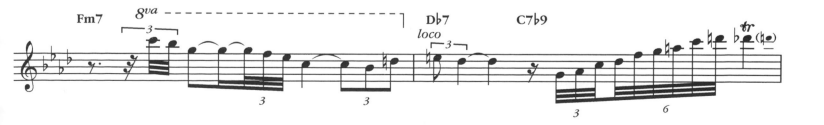

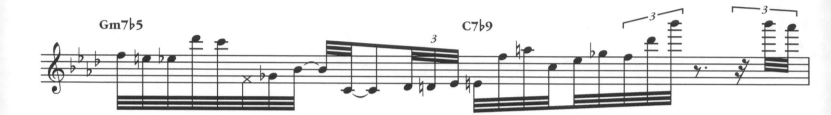

*play harmonic

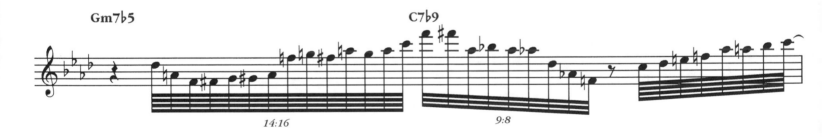

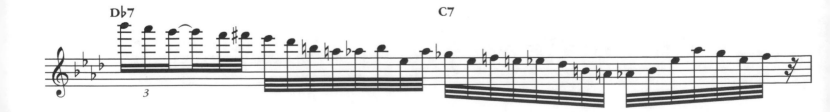

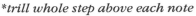

*trill whole step above each note

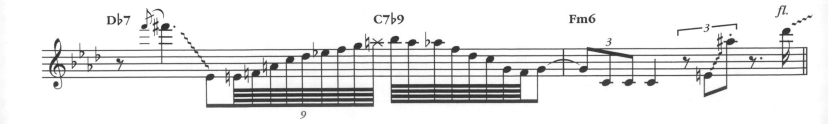

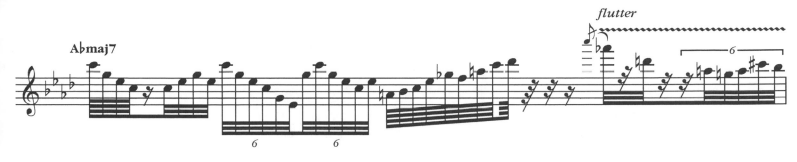

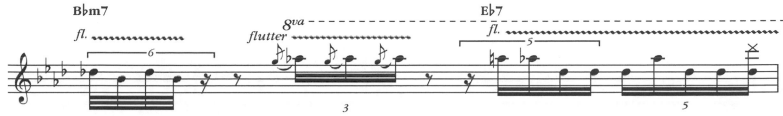

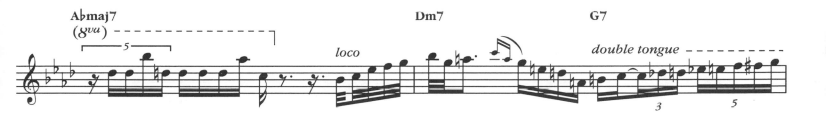

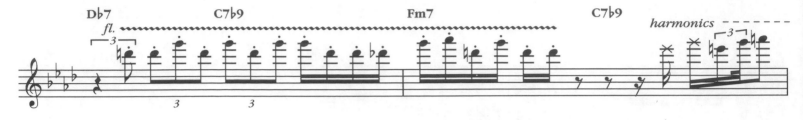

Cadenza